ABANDONED SOUTH CAROLINA

FORGOTTEN UPSTATE

LEXIS SANDERS AND
BREANNE HINSON

AMERICA
THROUGH TIME®
ADDING COLOR TO AMERICAN HISTORY

America Through Time is an imprint of Fonthill Media LLC
www.through-time.com
office@through-time.com

Published by Arcadia Publishing by arrangement with Fonthill Media LLC
For all general information, please contact Arcadia Publishing:
Telephone: 843-853-2070
Fax: 843-853-0044
E-mail: sales@arcadiapublishing.com
For customer service and orders:
Toll-Free 1-888-313-2665

www.arcadiapublishing.com

First published 2020

ISBN 978-1-63499-250-3

Typeset in Trade Gothic 10pt on 15pt
Printed and bound in England

CONTENTS

About the Authors **4**

Introduction **5**

1 Painted Wards and Creaking Floors **7**

2 Earth's Reclaimed Industrial Life **26**

3 Home Is Where the Hearth Is **66**

ABOUT THE AUTHORS

LEXIS SANDERS AND BREANNE HINSON maintain a balance of the creative arts, travel, work, and school. Lexis is currently going to school to earn her certification to be a veterinarian technician while doing art in her free time. Breanne is currently focused on earning a master's degree in zoology while writing her first dark fantasy novel. When time allows, the two search far and wide for new places to explore and take photographs of abandoned places for their side project, *ExplorationX*. Telling the stories of the places that once stood is just one of many of their passions.

INTRODUCTION

What started out as simple curiosity led to full-blown adventures hours away from our small city of Greenwood, South Carolina. South Carolina is rich with history; however, plenty of it was left to ruin without a second glance or thought. Unlike most, we found a sense of beauty in the world of decay. Earth, in our eyes, has a gift of making the lost artifacts of the past beautiful in a world full of repulsiveness. Our love for the decrepit has brought us into the loving and secretive community of urban exploring. We have spent hours at a time, and some sleepless nights, finding destinations and uncovering their past. Constant planning around tight schedules and budgets is what makes the task of exploring difficult. Yet, we continue to do so out of love for the old, leaving right at sunrise and returning far after sunset to reach these places hours away.

Many places are one of many left, whereas others are part of but a handful. It is a shame that due to national and local events, these structures have been left to fall. It is our goal as explorers to teach and educate the importance of preservation and history. Photographs are just a small way for us to preserve the past. Every day, our lives are enriched by many cultures, yet few seek the past that started it all. The past acts as the missing piece in the puzzle of who we are humans. And here in South Carolina, our past is filled with mills and plantations. These may not be the most glorious of things to be associated with, but they are still what made the culture of this state what it is today.

Leave only footprints, take only memories. This unspoken rule of exploring is vital in maintaining the abandoned world. For us, we not only take memories, but physical ones in the form of photographs to share with the world around us. As the world changes, every day a little bit of history, once a part of people's daily lives, is forgotten. What was once known as a daily job, a weekend family trip, and a faithful home for many years is now left to fade into nothingness. We seek to remember distant memories covered in dust. Here we share just a handful of the many photographs taken at numerous sites within the state of South Carolina. Due to these places no longer being safe and for the preservation of these sites, we will not be disclosing where in the state these places are, nor their names. And if it is known where these places are, we request all who visit to respect the one rule of exploring.

1

PAINTED WARDS AND CREAKING FLOORS

We walked through a portal made of cracked red brick and rotted wood. We jumped into a world filled with the past, leaving behind one filled with the future. The sun peered in occasionally, lighting dust kicked up by our slow feet, our eyes taking in what could be seen. The floorboards creaked beneath our feet as we shuffled along the rotting floors, fearful the water-damaged tiles would be unable to hold our weight. The air was thick and heavy, making us sweat. Dust clouded our vision into the far distance, dancing in the shine of our flashlights. The ghosts of the past hid as we began our ascent to the upper floors. The health facilities we've been to hold a special place within us, both emotionally and logically. Hospitals and mental asylums are well known in history as being some of the most grueling places ever to exist. Even though such facilities hold a bad reputation, there was good intention behind most of them.

South Carolina relies heavily on industrial infrastructure; thus, health issues were common amongst factory workers and their families. Although abandoned mills and factories far outnumber hospitals and mental asylums, these vacant facilities still exist. Many civilians suffered from diseases such as tuberculosis, brown lungs, disfiguration of the muscle and skeletons, and even several types of cancer. This is part of the reason why Greenwood, South Carolina, is home to one of the best genetic centers in the country.

The history of asylums is also rich in the state. South Carolina's past with mental asylums is dark. A few of the more prominent mental asylums were founded around the time of the Civil War and the Industrial Revolution. These few were well known for abusive and cruel treatment towards patients. Here, we show you just a handful of what remains of a couple of these infamous facilities.

The morning sun shines down upon the world with a warm welcome.

People forget, but the Earth does not.

Above: The sun breathes life back into the world of decay.

Left: Metal frames lie at rest, no longer used by man.

Bright walls became stripped away by stale air.

Any news heard within these walls no longer rings in the ears of many.

Above: When night falls, the Devil plays.

Left: Down the broken halls, memories of the dead walk.

Between these doors, many have walked with diseased lungs.

Murals of the past chip and fade with fleeting time.

Hidden halls hold treasures of the past.

Above: Wet floors become sticky with dust and debris.

Right: Industrial machinery litters the floor, moved from places by delinquent children.

Empty cabinets left open and damaged by careless looters.

Forgotten files slowly decay in sealed rooms.

Bitter emotions glossed over in hopes to bring joy in times of no cure.

Paint crumbles and peels as the building remains vacant of care.

Rusted knobs render doors useless for hiding the past.

Many memories scatter the floors and walls, forgotten by once loving families.

Empty halls filled with cabinets hold no sign of what was before.

Posters in many rooms were used to brighten the somber mood.

Left: Elevator shafts remain shut for eternity, held together by rust and debris.

Below: The sun shines through, illuminating what fallen lights cannot.

Above: Fleeting life leaves behind few capsules of time.

Right: Life becomes frozen in time, as if everything was dropped and left.

Water damage brings down tiles and eats away at what remains.

Black mold dots the past as water soaks the world.

Productivity no longer reigns as the facility closed its doors for good.

Busy bees no longer cleaned while the foolish destroyed property.

A wide room, once full of life, now sits quiet and lit only by sunlight.

The world stands silent as calls are no longer heard.

2

EARTH'S RECLAIMED INDUSTRIAL LIFE

The chill in the air bit our ears, only to be warmed again by the sun. The winter air held the mill as the sun cast its rays, creating defined shadows. The massive building, colored with reds and browns like the clay of earth, stood tall and solemn. Looking to the sky from the roof brought a sense of peace. The air was fresh and clean up top, whereas inside it was muggy and damp. Most of the floors had either fallen or were on the verge of doing so. They were soaked to the core with water and mold. Rot ate away at the inside of such a magnificent place that was once alive and teeming with workers. With the rustling wind, one could almost see the silhouettes of the worker bees that once treaded day after day through the halls.

Like most other Southern states with a history of mass cotton production, textile mills were extremely common in South Carolina. Textile mills are what the state thrived from, breathing life into such a rural area. South Carolina was built on factory-related industries. In many smaller cities or towns, you will often find nothing but mill villages, regardless of a mill's presence or lack of one. In our small city, there have been a good handful of textile factories in the past. Today, there only stands one that continues to run in Greenwood.

Many towns and cities either abandoned or tore down any mills after a massive decline in the American textile industry. Across the state, mills and modern factories alike are commonly found abandoned. Driving to our set destinations of known abandoned facilities, we have uncovered a large number of unnamed mills or modern factories that sit vacant on overgrown lots and cracked foundations. Some stand just barely visible and far from roads, while others sit directly off well-traveled highways or in the center of neighborhoods. It is unclear why some places closed, leaving us to assume it had to do with the financial instability found in the state. For other facilities, all it took was a quick internet search to find the reasons for closure.

Around the older mills, the remnants of life still exist. The homes that were once used for mill workers and their families are now the abodes of families who live their daily lives without the nearby plants.

The steps to success are long, but full of life.

Sitting lots, once full and bustling, are only greeted by the kiss of the sun.

Overgrown and broken, yet life carries on.

Many things block doors. Some are easier to bypass than others.

Danger can be found anywhere. Tread lightly on your endeavors.

To reach higher ground, you must first climb.

Right: At the end of every tunnel is a source of light.

Below left: When flames break out, they're put to rest shortly after.

Below right: Age can be told with a glimpse at the objects left to sit.

The collapse of an old world is a stunning display.

There is always the grim reminder that not everything can be saved.

Above: Power, once given, ceases to exist.

Right: Earth slowly reclaims what was once hers.

Left: Vines and weeds overgrow, left to hide away the past.

Below: A labyrinth made of ivy conceals the walls of the past.

Broken entryways make way for the homeless.

What once provided power, now provides shelter.

Life will eventually become anew atop the remains of the old.

The afternoon sun begins to set on a place of eternal rest.

Eventually, painted faces also fade away.

What was once a clean place is now a dirty home.

Water flowed through metal veins, bringing life to an empty shell.

Chipped paint and broken pipes make the organs of a rotting structure.

Right: The storms and rains of the past chip away at dirty paint.

Below: Complexity becomes simplicity after years of copper looters.

Above: The bright caution of yellow, now turned muddy red with time.

Left: Once fully rusted, things eventually crumble and fall apart.

Sheets of metal stand, holding together the last recognizable pieces of the past.

One man's trash is another man's treasure.

Above: The power of Earth once contained in such a simple design.

Left: As time moves, conditions will continue to deteriorate.

Right: As daylight dims, the shadows encase the lost.

Below: Energy is simple, yet to create it is beyond simplicity.

Above: With time, man follows with chaotic pastimes.

Left: Only small unreachable places are left to nature's grasps.

Above left: The world remains quiet above the chaos upon the ground.

Above right: A home for the restless, unaware of the past, is what becomes of these places.

Discarded and broken, tools used for safety become forgotten.

Busy bees no longer swarm empty hives full of danger.

The veins of life cover stone as if they were webs belonging to a spider.

Roots and leaves shelter the deceased.

The morning sun casts its rays, intensifying the emptiness felt within.

An open door is not always a welcoming one if mystery shrouds it.

Wildlife finds new uses for the things left behind.

What was once considered beautiful now lies stained and gutted.

Above: Unstable ground littered with fallen brick and stone in a room filled with pools of stagnant water.

Left: Water-soaked boards hold the floor beneath, unrecognizable.

Slimy brick covered in layers of dust and decay surround frozen doors.

Nameless machines sit empty and rusted.

Left: Brick becomes weather-worn with age.

Below: Airducts slowly fall to pieces as the floors above them begin to sag.

High-arched doorways leading to vast rooms welcome all who enter.

Mysterious machinery tower above, foreshadowing the unpredictable collapse.

Above: Hatches frozen in place make one question, just what made such a place run?

Left: The grays of winter begin to turn green once again.

Opposite: Broken glass overrun by vines basks in shadows.

Failing structures lead to unease.

Water damage becomes prevalent in the ceilings of wood.

Right: Rooms containing rusted parts are home to the waters of floods.

Below: Missing pieces, lost to time, never to be recovered.

Left: Breakers and boards sit empty, stripped of everything.

Below left: Even lost machinery begins to chip when left unkept.

Below right: The new world meets the old.

A breathtaking view of the world around, best seen through broken glass.

The floor begins to sink as the ceiling begins to break.

Dusty chains and dripping walls make the world just a little darker.

Right: Collection of dust and rust makes things just a little more fragile.

Below: The ceiling begins its timely descent.

Unused hydrants are left unchecked, disappearing behind small vines.

Broken windows go unnoticed as greenery becomes curtains.

3

HOME IS WHERE THE HEARTH IS

Even everyday life comes to an end as the winters warm and the summers fade. The homes that sit, tucked in corners, turn gray while schools fall and break. The summer days and nights shadow over old pools and hangout spots. The winter cradles old papers and paint. Old leaves crunch beneath our feet as we travel to faraway places. The smiling faces of families during dinner hide away. The giggling of students as they walk the halls fade into fallen walls. Sale pitches followed with signed papers fly in the wind through broken glass. These daily lives now sit overgrown with brush and greenery as we venture into the past of many people's lives.

The wind kissed our cheeks while the drizzling of rain chilled our bones. The innards of the walls had been torn and gutted, leaving nothing but drywall and rubble. The sound of the trees rustling outside filled our ears as we took in what remained of the home. Silently we crept through the halls, opening doors and peering in. Large webs filled corners and rooms, and bird nests nestled in cabinets and windowsills. This house—now vacant of people—is called home by wildlife. Moving on, we see graffiti painted concrete. Almost every square inch, it seemed, was covered with bright paint, courtesy of wild teens. Many summers had heated the high dive as people sat on it, smiling and waving to those below them. The world seemed joyful as everyone cooled in the massive pool. Life carried forward as the facility closed its doors. Green leaves of ivy and large pines grew, cracking and unsettling the foundation of the Olympic-sized pool.

Time moves forward as generations grow and pass, leaving footprints of their time in the ash. It is always the homes and tiny buildings that hold the most secrets or the most stories. Although larger abandoned sites such as hospitals and factories are more popular among the mass, we see that personal places like homes and schools have the most significance. Without these homes, people couldn't grow in rural areas. And without children or parents, there would be no past to have. Daily life holds the key to everything. There would be no history of these places if life had never come to flourish there.

There she stands by the window, gazing with solemn eyes.

Above: He sits patiently, admiring the life he had lived that now had come to pass.

Left: An empty home sits broken and unused.

Even the tallest and most victorious come crumbling back to the Earth below.

Many feet walked through these doors, without a second thought as to what would come.

Rooms, once separate, now come together as one space for the sun to smile upon.

Left: As ceilings crumble and bookshelves fall, dust-covered memories hold what was once seen as gold.

Below: Water seeps between, exposing the bones that hid underneath.

Above: Tiny cobwebs and little nests call what is old to us, new to them.

Right: The sands of time begin to sift as foundations begin to crumble beneath.

Left: Chapters and stories must end, but the memories still live.

Below: Brick and stone weather the storm, whereas wood does not.

The world is filled with madness, and solitude with serenity.

With an open roof, stained wood is kissed by rain and sun.

Webs and dust cling to their places, only to be swept away by the breath of wind.

Every good thing must come to an end.

Right: Rooms once filled with kids are now filled with rubble.

Below: New openings make room for new beginnings.

Lonely doors sit open to be greeted by the brush of wind.

A multitude of rooms now stand in extreme disrepair, never to be touched again.

Above: The walls of brick speak a history in a language none can understand.

Right: Painted walls become green with vines and leaves as time moves forward.

Above: Broken bones left to never heal nor stand ever again.

Left: The sun reaches out, painting the edges of chipped sills.

Crystal glass shattered, letting the outside world in.

Just across the street, the world ignores the lost.

A workplace for many now sits as an empty shell, cast aside.

Electricity is of in no need after looters had come about.

Dust quickly gathers on the few remnants left of a rotting shell.

Vandals seek gain in nothing but satisfaction.

Right: To play with the heart is to also play with the mind.

Below: The world seems small at a glance from a far distance, but quickly grows vast the closer you come to it.

Left: A mass of people at one moment were onlookers, watching the fun unfold.

Below: A world once free of green, now unable to be seen.

Before, life would jump. Now life clings.

Masses of young trees casts shadows upon the past.

The only sound of pattering feet now stems from curious faces.

Shallow pools belong to the young life that thrives.

As the world fades to gray, art keeps life going.

Above: The laughter and cries of joy fill old memories.

Left: What was once filled now runs dry.

Graffiti covered walls hide concrete from years before.

Above: Layers upon layers of paint become bleached by the sun.

Left: Weeds grow between the cracks of aged concrete.

Vines grow high upon broken walls.

Rusted doors sit ajar, fixed in place by growth and rust.

Fallen limbs shelter chipped paint from wind and rain.

Physical objects remain few in number as time goes on.

Right: Blue tiles hint to the life that once went on.

Below: Only the skeleton of this home remains in place to this day.

Metal frames, bent and broken, act like portals into a new world of curiosity.